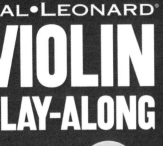

HAL•LEONARD®
VIOLIN
PLAY-ALONG

AUDIO
ACCESS
INCLUDED

VOL. 49

ROCK *Favorites*

To access audio visit:
www.halleonard.com/mylibrary

Enter Code
6340-2977-5183-8340

Jerry Loughney, violin
Angela Schmidt, cello, viola, and additional violin
Tom Crowell, electric and acoustic guitars
Dan Maske, keyboards, drumset, and brass
Recorded and Produced by Dan Maske

ISBN 978-1-4803-9545-9

HAL•LEONARD®
CORPORATION
7777 W. BLUEMOUND RD. P.O. BOX 13819 MILWAUKEE, WI 53213

For all works contained herein:
Unauthorized copying, arranging, adapting, recording, Internet posting, public performance,
or other distribution of the printed or recorded music in this publication is an infringement of copyright.
Infringers are liable under the law.

Visit Hal Leonard Online at
www.halleonard.com

Good Riddance
(Time of Your Life)

Words by Billie Joe
Music by Green Day

Moderately

acoustic guitar

© 1997 WB MUSIC CORP. and GREEN DAZE MUSIC
All Rights Administered by WB MUSIC CORP.
All Rights Reserved   Used by Permission

Kashmir

Words and Music by Jimmy Page, Robert Plant and John Bonham

Heavy Orchestral Rock

© 1975 (Renewed) FLAMES OF ALBION MUSIC, INC.
All Rights Administered by WB MUSIC CORP.
All Rights Reserved   Used by Permission

My Immortal

Words and Music by Ben Moody, Amy Lee and David Hodges

© 2003 BMG RIGHTS MANAGEMENT (IRELAND) LTD., ZOMBIES ATE MY PUBLISHING and FOR THE FALLEN PUBLISHING
All Rights Administered by CHRYSALIS ONE SONGS and BMG RIGHTS MANAGEMENT (US) LLC
All Rights Reserved   Used by Permission

Overture

Words and Music by Jacob Pitts, Jeremy Ferguson,
John William Feldmann, Andrew Biersack and Ashley Purdy

© 2012 ATLANTIC RECORDS ASCAP PUB DESIGNEE, ABIERSACK, JAKE PITTS MUSIC, JINXXED FOR LIFE MUSIC,
ASHLEY PURDY MUSIC, SONGS OF RED BULL (ASCAP) and ROBOT DRAGON MUSIC (ASCAP)
All Rights for ATLANTIC RECORDS ASCAP PUB DESIGNEE, ABIERSACK, JAKE PITTS MUSIC,
JINXXED FOR LIFE MUSIC and ASHLEY PURDY MUSIC Administered by WB MUSIC CORP.
All Rights for ROBOT DRAGON MUSIC Administered by SONGS OF RED BULL
All Rights Reserved   Used by Permission

Game of Thrones

Theme From The HBO Series GAME OF THRONES

Music by Ramin Djawadi

Copyright © 2011 TL MUSIC PUBLISHING
All Rights Controlled and Administered by UNIVERSAL MUSIC CORP.
All Rights Reserved   Used by Permission

Say Something

Words and Music by Ian Axel, Chad Vaccarino and Mike Campbell

Copyright © 2011 SONGS OF UNIVERSAL, INC., IAN AXEL MUSIC, CHAD VACCARINO PUBLISHING and SONGTRUST BLVD.
All Rights for IAN AXEL MUSIC and CHAD VACCARINO PUBLISHING Controlled and Administered by SONGS OF UNIVERSAL, INC.
All Rights Reserved   Used by Permission

Skyfall

from the Motion Picture SKYFALL
Words and Music by Adele Adkins and Paul Epworth

Copyright © 2012 MELTED STONE PUBLISHING LTD. and EMI MUSIC PUBLISHING LTD.
All Rights for MELTED STONE PUBLISHING LTD. in the U.S. and Canada Controlled and Administered by
UNIVERSAL - SONGS OF POLYGRAM INTERNATIONAL, INC.
All Rights for EMI MUSIC PUBLISHING LTD. in the U.S. and Canada Controlled and Administered by EMI APRIL MUSIC INC.
All Rights Reserved   Used by Permission

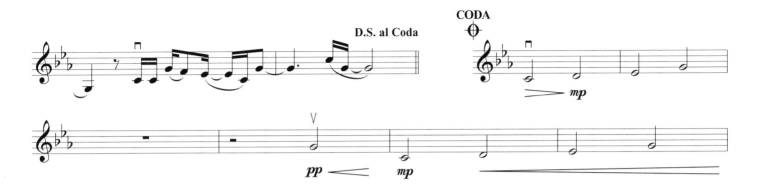

D.S. al Coda

CODA

Viva la Vida

Words and Music by Guy Berryman, Jon Buckland, Will Champion and Chris Martin

Copyright © 2008 by Universal Music Publishing MGB Ltd.
All Rights in the United States and Canada Administered by Universal Music - MGB Songs
International Copyright Secured   All Rights Reserved

The Violin Play-Along Series

Play your favorite songs quickly and easily!

Just follow the music, listen to the CD or online audio to hear how the violin should sound, and then play along using the separate backing tracks. The audio files are enhanced so you can adjust the recordings to any tempo without changing pitch!

1. Bluegrass
00842152 Book/CD Pack $14.99

2. Popular Songs
00842153 Book/CD Pack $14.99

3. Classical
00842154 Book/CD Pack $14.99

4. Celtic
00842155 Book/CD Pack $14.99

5. Christmas Carols
00842156 Book/CD Pack $14.99

6. Holiday Hits
00842157 Book/CD Pack $14.99

7. Jazz
00842196 Book/CD Pack $14.99

8. Country Classics
00842230 Book/CD Pack $12.99

9. Country Hits
00842231 Book/CD Pack $14.99

10. Bluegrass Favorites
00842232 Book/CD Pack $14.99

11. Bluegrass Classics
00842233 Book/CD Pack $14.99

12. Wedding Classics
00842324 Book/CD Pack $14.99

13. Wedding Favorites
00842325 Book/CD Pack $14.99

14. Blues Classics
00842427 Book/CD Pack $14.99

15. Stephane Grappelli
00842428 Book/CD Pack $14.99

16. Folk Songs
00842429 Book/CD Pack $14.99

17. Christmas Favorites
00842478 Book/CD Pack $14.99

18. Fiddle Hymns
00842499 Book/CD Pack $14.99

19. Lennon & McCartney
00842564 Book/CD Pack $14.99

20. Irish Tunes
00842565 Book/CD Pack $14.99

21. Andrew Lloyd Webber
00842566 Book/CD Pack $14.99

22. Broadway Hits
00842567 Book/CD Pack $14.99

23. Pirates of the Caribbean
00842625 Book/CD Pack $14.99

24. Rock Classics
00842640 Book/CD Pack $14.99

25. Classical Masterpieces
00842642 Book/CD Pack $14.99

26. Elementary Classics
00842643 Book/CD Pack $14.99

27. Classical Favorites
00842646 Book/CD Pack $14.99

28. Classical Treasures
00842647 Book/CD Pack $14.99

29. Disney Favorites
00842648 Book/CD Pack $14.99

30. Disney Hits
00842649 Book/CD Pack $14.99

31. Movie Themes
00842706 Book/CD Pack $14.99

32. Favorite Christmas Songs
00102110 Book/CD Pack $14.99

33. Hoedown
00102161 Book/CD Pack $14.99

34. Barn Dance
00102568 Book/CD Pack $14.99

35. Lindsey Stirling
00109715 Book/CD Pack $19.99

36. Hot Jazz
00110373 Book/CD Pack $14.99

37. Taylor Swift
00116361 Book/CD Pack $14.99

38. John Williams
00116367 Book/CD Pack $14.99

39. Italian Songs
00116368 Book/CD Pack $14.99

41. Johann Strauss
00121041 Book/CD Pack $14.99

42. Light Classics
00121935 Book/Online Audio $14.99

43. Light Orchestra Pop
00122126 Book/Online Audio $14.99

44. French Songs
00122123 Book/Online Audio $14.99

45. Lindsey Stirling Hits
00123128 Book/Online Audio $19.99

47. Light Masterworks
00124149 Book/Online Audio $14.99

48. Frozen
00126478 Book/Online Audio $14.99

49. Pop/Rock
00130216 Book/Online Audio $14.99

50. Songs For Beginners
00131417 Book/Online Audio $14.99

51. Chart Hits For Beginners
00131418 Book/Online Audio $14.99

Disney characters and artwork © Disney Enterprises, Inc.
Prices, contents, and availability
subject to change without notice.

7777 W. BLUEMOUND RD. P.O. BOX 13819 MILWAUKEE, WI 53213

www.halleonard.com

0315

HAL•LEONARD
INSTRUMENTAL
PLAY-ALONG

Your favorite songs are arranged just for solo instrumentalists with this outstanding series. Each book includes a great full-accompaniment play-along CD so you can sound just like a pro! Check out **www.halleonard.com** to see all the titles available.

Disney Greats

Arabian Nights • Hawaiian Roller Coaster Ride • It's a Small World • Look Through My Eyes • Yo Ho (A Pirate's Life for Me) • and more.

_____ 00841934	Flute	$12.95
_____ 00841935	Clarinet	$12.95
_____ 00841936	Alto Sax	$12.95
_____ 00841937	Tenor Sax	$12.95
_____ 00841938	Trumpet	$12.95
_____ 00841939	Horn	$12.95
_____ 00841940	Trombone	$12.95
_____ 00841941	Violin	$12.95
_____ 00841942	Viola	$12.95
_____ 00841943	Cello	$12.95
_____ 00842078	Oboe	$12.95

Great Themes

Bella's Lullaby • Chariots of Fire • Get Smart • Hawaii Five-O Theme • I Love Lucy • The Odd Couple • Spanish Flea • and more.

_____ 00842468	Flute	$12.99
_____ 00842469	Clarinet	$12.99
_____ 00842470	Alto Sax	$12.99
_____ 00842471	Tenor Sax	$12.99
_____ 00842472	Trumpet	$12.99
_____ 00842473	Horn	$12.99
_____ 00842474	Trombone	$12.99
_____ 00842475	Violin	$12.99
_____ 00842476	Viola	$12.99
_____ 00842477	Cello	$12.99

Coldplay

Clocks • Every Teardrop Is a Waterfall • Fix You • In My Place • Lost! • Paradise • The Scientist • Speed of Sound • Trouble • Violet Hill • Viva La Vida • Yellow.

_____ 00103337	Flute	$12.99
_____ 00103338	Clarinet	$12.99
_____ 00103339	Alto Sax	$12.99
_____ 00103340	Tenor Sax	$12.99
_____ 00103341	Trumpet	$12.99
_____ 00103342	Horn	$12.99
_____ 00103343	Trombone	$12.99
_____ 00103344	Violin	$12.99
_____ 00103345	Viola	$12.99
_____ 00103346	Cello	$12.99

Popular Hits

Breakeven • Fireflies • Halo • Hey, Soul Sister • I Gotta Feeling • I'm Yours • Need You Now • Poker Face • Viva La Vida • You Belong with Me • and more.

_____ 00842511	Flute	$12.99
_____ 00842512	Clarinet	$12.99
_____ 00842513	Alto Sax	$12.99
_____ 00842514	Tenor Sax	$12.99
_____ 00842515	Trumpet	$12.99
_____ 00842516	Horn	$12.99
_____ 00842517	Trombone	$12.99
_____ 00842518	Violin	$12.99
_____ 00842519	Viola	$12.99
_____ 00842520	Cello	$12.99

Lennon & McCartney Favorites

All You Need Is Love • A Hard Day's Night • Here, There and Everywhere • Hey Jude • Let It Be • Nowhere Man • Penny Lane • She Loves You • When I'm Sixty-Four • and more.

_____ 00842600	Flute	$12.99
_____ 00842601	Clarinet	$12.99
_____ 00842602	Alto Sax	$12.99
_____ 00842603	Tenor Sax	$12.99
_____ 00842604	Trumpet	$12.99
_____ 00842605	Horn	$12.99
_____ 00842606	Trombone	$12.99
_____ 00842607	Violin	$12.99
_____ 00842608	Viola	$12.99
_____ 00842609	Cello	$12.99

Women of Pop

Bad Romance • Jar of Hearts • Mean • My Life Would Suck Without You • Our Song • Rolling in the Deep • Single Ladies (Put a Ring on It) • Teenage Dream • and more.

_____ 00842650	Flute	$12.99
_____ 00842651	Clarinet	$12.99
_____ 00842652	Alto Sax	$12.99
_____ 00842653	Tenor Sax	$12.99
_____ 00842654	Trumpet	$12.99
_____ 00842655	Horn	$12.99
_____ 00842656	Trombone	$12.99
_____ 00842657	Violin	$12.99
_____ 00842658	Viola	$12.99
_____ 00842659	Cello	$12.99

Movie Music

And All That Jazz • Come What May • I Am a Man of Constant Sorrow • I Believe I Can Fly • I Walk the Line • Seasons of Love • Theme from *Spider Man* • and more.

_____ 00842090	Clarinet	$10.95
_____ 00842091	Alto Sax	$10.95
_____ 00842092	Tenor Sax	$10.95
_____ 00842094	Horn	$10.95
_____ 00842095	Trombone	$10.95
_____ 00842096	Violin	$10.95
_____ 00842097	Viola	$10.95

TV Favorites

The Addams Family Theme • The Brady Bunch • Green Acres Theme • Happy Days • Johnny's Theme • Linus and Lucy • Theme from the Simpsons • and more.

_____ 00842079	Flute	$10.95
_____ 00842080	Clarinet	$10.95
_____ 00842081	Alto Sax	$10.95
_____ 00842082	Tenor Sax	$10.95
_____ 00842083	Trumpet	$10.95
_____ 00842084	Horn	$10.95
_____ 00842085	Trombone	$10.95
_____ 00842087	Viola	$10.95

Wicked

As Long As You're Mine • Dancing Through Life • Defying Gravity • For Good • I'm Not That Girl • Popular • The Wizard and I • and more.

_____ 00842236	Flute	$11.95
_____ 00842237	Clarinet	$11.95
_____ 00842238	Alto Saxophone	$11.95
_____ 00842239	Tenor Saxophone	$11.95
_____ 00842240	Trumpet	$11.95
_____ 00842241	Horn	$11.95
_____ 00842242	Trombone	$11.95
_____ 00842243	Violin	$11.95
_____ 00842244	Viola	$11.95
_____ 00842245	Cello	$11.95

FOR MORE INFORMATION, SEE YOUR LOCAL MUSIC DEALER, OR WRITE TO:

HAL•LEONARD®
CORPORATION

7777 W. BLUEMOUND RD. P.O. BOX 13819 MILWAUKEE, WI 53213

Prices, contents, and availability subject to change without notice.
Disney characters and artwork © Disney Enterprises, Inc.

0315